CHICKEN
CLASSICS

The Best
And The Brightest
The Bird
At Its Finest

CHICKEN CLASSICS

Chicken
Masterpieces
From
Around
The
World

Patricia Stapley

ILLUSTRATIONS BY
Jennie Oppenheimer

HEARST BOOKS
New York

Library of Congress Cataloging-in-Publication Data
Stapley, Patricia.
Chicken classics: chicken masterpieces from around the world /
by Patricia Stapley: illustrations by Jennie Oppenheimer —
1st ed.
p. cm
ISBN: 0-688-12414-3
1. Cookery (Chicken). 2. Cookery, International. I. Title.
TX750.5.C45S73 1994
641.6'65 — dc20   93-41978
CIP
Printed in Singapore

First Edition

1 3 5 7 9 10 8 6 4 2

F Y
PRODUCTIONS

For
Alice Olivia Hill

CONTENTS

Chicken
Here & There

Wonderful chicken is like a blank canvas, showing off herbs and spices to their best advantage. It's remarkable to see how every cuisine in every country has its own classic chicken dish. The recipes in *Chicken Classics* are showcase examples of these signature flavors and classic cooking techniques.

Chicken Classics contains nineteen recipes. I chose these recipes because of their unique combination of flavors and for their interesting and useful preparations. Three are my favorite American specialties, gumbo from Louisiana, fried chicken from Kentucky, and chicken baked in paper from my home state, California. The other sixteen recipes, some old friends, some new and unusual, come together for a culinary trip around the world that starts in Europe with the famous French wine-based stew, Coq au Vin, travels to Africa for an exotic Phyllo Torte from Egypt, and moves on to the busiest city in the world, Tokyo, for Yakitori Chicken, the fun fast food on skewers. To heighten your sense of place, I added an à la carte menu for each country to suggest typical accompaniments and beverages.

Chicken has it all! It's easily prepared, widely available,

and reasonably priced. Each recipe specifies the kind of chicken that best suits it: for example, fryers for the all-American Fried Chicken With Gravy or cut-up broilers for seasoning with a tasty basting of yakitori sauce. Both broilers and fryers are good for steaming and poaching, too. Roasting chickens and capons (neutered roosters) are destined for cooking in the oven. With more meat per pound than the smaller fryers or broilers, roasters are just right for an Italian Roast Chicken or honey-glazed baked chicken from Portugal. Stewing chickens are the most flavorful and can stand up to the long, slow cooking demanded by soups and stews. Not so good for roasting because they tend to be older, tougher birds, stewers produce a strong, rich broth perfect for Chicken and Dumplings or Cock-a-Leekie.

Organic produce and free-range poultry are now widely available in supermarkets and farmers' markets. I believe that free-range chickens are the wave of the future for reasons of taste as well as for health considerations, but the choice is yours: You can easily substitute the versatile packaged fryer or broiler in the preparation of free-range chicken baked in paper.

Wherever you purchase poultry, look for creamy yellow or white skin that's supple and plump. Check carefully for any undesirable discoloration, blemishes, or bruises. Also, trust your nose to tell you if a bird is fresh. If you buy mass-packaged chicken, check the expiration date that by law must appear somewhere on the label.

If you are cooking the chicken right away, unwrap it, rinse it carefully in cold water, and pat it dry. I like to refresh the bird by squeezing fresh lemon juice over the skin. If you don't plan to use it right away, rewrap it loosely in plastic or waxed paper and store it in the coldest part of the refrigerator. Refrigerated chicken should be cooked within two days. I recommend buying chicken the same day you plan to cook it. If you decide to freeze chicken, unwrap it, rinse under cold water, pat dry, and rewrap it in heavy plastic wrap or place it in a freezer bag. Whole chicken will keep up to three months in the freezer. Never refreeze defrosted chicken.

The recipes in *Chicken Classics* were developed to serve four to six people, but they can easily be increased to serve a larger group. I like to cook more than I need, because there's nothing better then leftover chicken the next day for lunch or a pot-luck dinner.

Whether you roast it whole in the dry heat of the oven or combine several steps such as rapid browning followed by gentle stewing to develop the flavors, chicken reigns supreme as the world's premier main dish ingredient.

Europe

ITALY

Roast Chicken

~ classic complements ~

A LA CARTE

Spiedini Romana

Fusilli Puttanesca Blanca

Tiramisù

Orvieto

ITALY

Roast Chicken

Roast Chicken Italian style is a simple classic. Dressed with a sprig of frisky fresh rosemary tucked under each wing and finished with a shower of lemon juice over the crisped golden skin, the bird comes out super juicy every time.

MAKES SIX SERVINGS

5-pound roasting chicken or capon	1 celery stalk, coarsely chopped
4 cloves garlic, crushed	5 sprigs fresh rosemary
1 small onion, cut into quarters	Salt and freshly ground black pepper to taste
1 medium carrot, coarsely chopped	2 tablespoons olive oil
	1 lemon, cut in half

Preheat the oven to 375° F.

Rinse the chicken under cold water. Pat dry.

Fill the cavity with the garlic, onion, carrot, and celery. Add three sprigs of rosemary. Sprinkle with salt and pepper and drizzle with one teaspoon of the olive oil.

Truss the chicken for roasting: Wind white cotton kitchen twine around the legs to tie them together and hold them close to the body. Rub two teaspoons of the olive oil over the outside of the bird. Season with salt and pepper. Slip a sprig of fresh rosemary under each wing.

4

Coat the bottom of the roasting pan with the remaining one tablespoon olive oil. Place the chicken on its side in the pan. Roast for fifteen minutes.

Turn the bird over to the opposite side, being careful not to puncture the skin. Baste with the cooking juices. Roast for fifteen minutes. Turn the chicken again, breast side up and baste. Roast for one hour.

Fifteen minutes before the hour is up, baste one last time. The chicken is done when the internal temperature of the thigh meat registers 165° F. on a cooking thermometer.

Remove the chicken from the oven. While it's still piping hot, squeeze the lemon juice all over it. Allow the bird to cool in the pan for ten minutes before transferring to a large serving platter. Unwind the kitchen twine and discard.

Transfer the pan to the stove top. Cook the roasting juices over high heat until slightly thickened, about two minutes. Pour the delicious juices through a strainer directly into a warmed gravy boat.

Carve the chicken at the table to serve family style. *Mangia!*

FRANCE

Coq au Vin

~ classic complements ~

A LA CARTE

Scallop Vinaigrette

Crusty Herb Baguette

Chocolate Mousse

Sparkling Anise Mineral Water

Coq au Vin

The French, with their love of good wine, turn simple poultry into a sophisticated stew. Onions, mushrooms, pungent garlic, and chicken steeped in wine — a savory delight.

M A K E S   F O U R   S E R V I N G S

3 1/2-pound frying chicken, cut into 8 pieces

6 slices bacon, cut into 1-inch pieces

Salt and freshly ground black pepper to taste

1/2 cup finely chopped onion

3 cloves garlic, finely chopped

2 carrots, cut into 1-inch rounds

1 celery stalk, cut into 1-inch pieces

1 large tomato, chopped

1/3 cup brandy

1/2 teaspoon dried thyme

1 bay leaf

3 cups red wine

4 slices firm white bread, crusts removed

1 1/2 tablespoons olive oil

20 pearl onions

1 teaspoon sugar

1/2 cup water

1 pound mushrooms caps, cut into quarters

2 tablespoons chopped fresh parsley

Rinse the chicken pieces under cold water. Pat dry.

In a large skillet, lightly brown the bacon over low heat. Set aside to drain on paper towels.

Turn up the heat under the same skillet to medium and brown the chicken on all sides, about ten minutes. Remove from the pan and season with salt and pepper.

8

Sauté the chopped onion and garlic in the fat remaining in the skillet until lightly browned. Add the carrots and celery and cook for two minutes. Add the tomato, brandy, thyme, bacon, and bay leaf. Stir to combine. Add the chicken. Pour in the wine and simmer, covered, for thirty minutes.

Preheat the oven to 400° F. for toasting the croutons. Slice each piece of bread in half on the diagonal to make eight triangles. Cut out "Vs" from the long sides of the slices to approximate heart shapes. Brush olive oil front and back. Arrange on a cookie sheet and toast until golden, about three minutes.

Meanwhile, fill a medium saucepan with water and bring to a boil. Cut a small cross in the bottom of each pearl onion. Place in the boiling water, lower the heat, and simmer for five minutes. Drain, rinse under cold water, and peel.

In a medium saucepan, combine the pearl onions with one tablespoon of the oil, the sugar, and water. Cook over high heat to boil off the liquid, sautéing the onions until glazed tender, about fifteen minutes. Stir in the mushrooms and sauté for two minutes. Remove from the heat, cover, and set aside.

Remove the chicken from the skillet and place on a large platter. Cover the chicken loosely to keep it warm. Turn up the heat under the skillet. Cook the sauce until it thickens, about ten minutes.

Spoon the mushrooms and pearl onions over the chicken. Ladle sauce over all. Dip each crouton in a bit of sauce and then in chopped parsley and arrange to fan the rim of the platter. Garnish with the remaining parsley.

SCOTLAND

Cock-a-Leekie

~classic complements~

A LA CARTE

Smoked Trout Paté

Homemade Cracked Grain Bread

Goat Cheese Crumbles On Raw Fennel

Strawberry Rhubarb Custard

Cock-a-Leekie

From the hearth of a West Country kitchen comes everyone's favorite chicken classic, chicken soup. The lyrically named Scottish variation, Cock-a-Leekie (literal translation: chicken and leeks) is a tasty crossing of mellow chicken, biting-but-good leeks, nutty-flavored rice, and a savory surprise of fruit-sweet prunes.

M A K E S   S I X   S E R V I N G S

3 1/2-pound stewing chicken

About 12 cups water

2/3 cup long-grain rice

Salt and freshly ground black pepper to taste

6 leeks

2 tablespoons olive oil

1 cup pitted prunes

1/2 cup chopped fresh parsley

Rinse the chicken under cold water.

Place the bird in a large heavy-bottomed pot. Add water to cover. Twelve cups should be about right; the idea is to use just enough to cover the chicken. Bring to a boil. Add the rice, salt, and pepper. Lower the heat and simmer gently, partially covered, for an hour and fifteen minutes.

Meanwhile, trim the leeks, leaving an inch of the firm green tops. Rinse them very well under cold running water to remove all the sandy grit trapped in the vegetable's tightly layered center. Slice the leeks into one-inch rounds.

12

In a sauté pan, warm the olive oil over medium heat. Sauté the leeks until they wilt, an excellent way to intensify the flavor of the vegetable, about three to four minutes. Set aside.

When the chicken has cooked for an hour and fifteen minutes, add the leeks and prunes. Continue to simmer the Cock-a-Leekie, partially covered, for forty-five minutes, or until the chicken is tender. The bird is done when a fork slides easily in and out of the thigh meat.

Turn off the heat. Carefully lift the chicken out of the pot and set it aside to cool to room temperature.

Skim the excess fat off the surface of the soup.

Remove the chicken skin, carve the meat off the bone, and cut into bite-size pieces. Return the chicken chunks to the soup. Simmer over low heat to reheat, about five minutes. Taste for salt and pepper.

Ladle the steaming cock-a-leekie into deep soup bowls. Garnish each portion with a generous sprinkling of the parsley.

ENGLAND

Chicken Pot Pie

~ classic complements ~

A LA CARTE

Greengage Pears & Limestone Lettuce

Brussels Sprouts Tossed With Shaved Stilton

Caramel Parfait

Fumé Blanc

Chicken Pot Pie

These chicken pot pies are not the usual bland fare. The key to an unexpected kick of extra flavor is the licorice-like herb tarragon. Each tasty pie sports a top hat of flaky puff pastry to ensure juiciness and to seal in the fresh snap of the gutsy garden vegetables.

M A K E S   F O U R   I N D I V I D U A L   P I E S

2 chicken breasts, skinned

2 1/2 cups chicken stock

3 sprigs fresh tarragon

2 carrots, peeled and cut into 1/4-inch rounds

1/2 cup shelled green peas (1/4 pound unshelled)

16 pearl onions, peeled

2 tablespoons unsalted butter

2 tablespoons all-purpose flour

1/4 cup heavy cream

Salt and freshly ground black pepper to taste

1 to 2 sheets frozen puff pastry, thawed

Rinse the chicken breasts under cold water.

In a medium skillet, combine one cup of the stock, the chicken, and one sprig tarragon. Cover and simmer for thirty minutes. Remove the chicken. Reserve the liquid. Discard the tarragon. Bone the chicken. Slice into bite-size pieces. Set aside.

In a small saucepan, combine one cup stock, the carrots, and one sprig tarragon. Bring to a boil. Cook for four minutes. Remove the carrots and set aside. Reserve the liquid. Discard the tarragon.

16

In a small saucepan, boil two cups of water. Blanch the peas for thirty seconds. Strain and add to the carrots.

Cut a small cross in the bottom of each pearl onion. In a small saucepan, boil the onions until tender. Drain, rinse under cold water, and peel. Add to the carrots and peas.

Melt the butter in a medium saucepan. Whisk in the flour. Cook over medium-low heat for three minutes. Add the reserved liquids, the remaining one-half cup stock, and the cream. Cook, whisking briskly, until the sauce comes to a boil and thickens. Toss in one sprig tarragon, remove from the heat, cover, and set aside to cool.

Butter four one-and-a-half-cup ramekins or baking dishes. Divide the chicken equally among them and scatter the vegetables over and around the chicken. Pour in sauce to cover.

To make the pastry tops: Place the pastry sheet on a work surface. Cut the dough into pieces that snugly cover the top of each ramekin. If the ramekins you use are round or square, one pastry sheet is enough to make four tops. If they are oval or rectangular, you will need two pastry sheets to cut out four pie covers. Set a pastry cap on top of each filled ramekin. Chill in the freezer for twenty minutes before baking.

Preheat the oven to 400° F.

Place the pot pies in the oven. Bake until the pastry is well browned, about thirty minutes. Let cool for five minutes before serving.

GERMANY

Chicken And Dumplings

~ classic complements ~

A LA CARTE

Chicken Liver Salad

Tarragon Tomatoes With Spinach Sour Cream

Black Forest Cake

Rhein Lager

Chicken And Dumplings

Nothing is more comforting on a chilled-to-the-bone day than that humble basic Chicken And Dumpling stew. A lazy simmer in the sweet-and-savory broth gives the parsley-flecked dumplings their maximum chicken flavor.

MAKES FOUR SERVINGS

3 1/2-pound stewing chicken, cut into 8 pieces

1/2 teaspoon salt, plus a pinch

1/2 teaspoon freshly ground black pepper

2 teaspoons paprika

1 tablespoon vegetable oil

1 small onion, sliced

2 leeks, white parts only, well rinsed and thinly sliced

1 stalk celery, coarsely chopped

1 large carrot, coarsely chopped

4 cups chicken stock

2 cups plus 3 tablespoons all-purpose flour

1 tablespoon plus 1 teaspoon baking powder

1/4 cup minced fresh parsley, plus 4 sprigs for garnish

5 tablespoons solid vegetable shortening

2 large eggs

2/3 cup milk

3 tablespoons butter

Rinse the chicken under cold water. Pat dry. Season with the half teaspoon of salt, the pepper, and paprika.

In a heavy-bottomed pot with a tightly fitting lid, heat the oil over high heat. Brown the chicken until golden on all sides, about ten minutes. Carefully pour off the cooking fat.

Add the onion, leeks, celery, carrot, and stock. Bring to a

boil. Lower the heat, cover, and simmer until the chicken is tender, about forty minutes.

While the chicken is stewing make the dumpling batter. In a large bowl, stir to combine two cups flour, the baking powder, pinch of salt, and minced parsley. Add the vegetable shortening. Use a pastry cutter or your fingertips to blend the dough to the consistency of oatmeal. Stir in the eggs and milk. Mix until the dough is evenly moistened. Cover and set aside. Remove the chicken and vegetables from the stock and place them on a large platter to cool slightly. Then skin and bone the chicken and shred into bite-size pieces. Set aside.

In a small saucepan, melt the butter over medium heat. Stir in the three tablespoons flour. Cook, stirring, until well blended, about three minutes.

Add the buttery flour to the stock. Whisk to combine completely. Simmer over low heat until the stock begins to thicken, about three minutes.

Drop rounded tablespoons of the batter into the simmering stock. The batter yields twelve to sixteen spoon-size dumplings. Cover the pot. Cook until the dumplings double in size and a toothpick inserted into the center of a dumpling comes out clean, about ten to fifteen minutes.

To serve, place the chicken and vegetables in four wide shallow bowls and top each serving with three to four dumplings. Ladle in broth to just cover. Garnish with the fresh parsley sprigs.

RUSSIA

Chicken Kiev

~classic complements~

A LA CARTE

Beet Borscht

Red Potatoes With Caviar & Sour Cream

Cherry Blini

Frozen Buffalo Grass Vodka

Chicken Kiev

Golden brown and crunchy on the outside, these delicious croquettes are tender and succulent on the inside. The first bite begins with the famous squirt of herb-infused butter. These treats are not as "naughty" as they might be if cooked in the traditional way. Instead of being deep fried, they're baked in the oven; not to worry, they're still plenty rich.

MAKES FOUR SERVINGS

4 tablespoons unsalted butter, at room temperature

2 cloves garlic, minced

3 tablespoons minced fresh parsley

2 tablespoons minced fresh chives

1 tablespoon freshly squeezed lemon juice

2 skinless, boneless chicken breasts, cut in half

Salt and freshly ground black pepper to taste

Pinch of cayenne pepper

1/3 cup all-purpose flour

1 large egg, beaten

1 cup fine bread crumbs

3 tablespoons olive oil

Combine the butter, garlic, parsley, chives, and lemon juice in a deep bowl. Mash together with a fork until well blended. Place the herb butter in the center of a sheet of plastic wrap. Fold the wrap over once to cover the butter. Mold the butter into a two-and-one-half-inch cylinder, about an inch thick. Roll it up in the plastic. Chill in the freezer for at least thirty minutes.

24

Rinse the chicken breasts under cold water. Pat dry.

Sandwich the breasts between sheets of wax paper, then flatten with a mallet or the flat side of a heavy knife until the meat is one eighth inch thick. Season with salt and pepper and cayenne. Set aside.

Remove the plastic wrap from the chilled butter cylinder. Slice it lengthwise into four equal pieces. Place one piece across the center of each breast. To form the breast into a croquette, fold over the sides to overlap. Roll each breast up from the bottom to completely enclose the butter. Press the seam down firmly to seal in the butter.

Dust each croquette generously with flour, dip in the beaten egg, and roll in the bread crumbs. Wrap each one in plastic wrap and refrigerate for four hours.

Preheat the oven to 350° F.

In a large heavy-bottomed skillet, heat the olive oil over medium heat. Sauté the croquettes until golden brown on all sides, about ten minutes. Be careful not to puncture the meat or the butter inside will escape. Remove the croquettes from the skillet. Set aside on paper towels for a minute or two to soak up excess oil before placing them on a cookie sheet to finish cooking in the oven. Bake about twenty minutes. To test for doneness, use the back of a fork to press down gently on the croquettes. If firm, they're cooked to perfection.

Chicken Kiev is so rich, one crisp chicken breast will satisfy even the heartiest appetite.

PORTUGAL

Baked Chicken

~ classic complements ~

A LA CARTE

Anchovy & Olive Tapenade On Grilled Bread

Caldo Verde

Ripe Pears & Fire-Roasted Almonds

Port Sangria

Baked Chicken

Portuguese cooking is gateway cuisine. Sweet-and-sour chicken, glaze-baked with a provocative blend of honey, lemon zest, and saffron, is a marvelous way to sample a typical chicken classic from the country where West meets East at dinnertime.

MAKES FOUR SERVINGS

3 1/2-pound roasting chicken, quartered

Salt and freshly ground pepper to taste

2 tablespoons olive oil

1 small red onion, finely chopped

3 cloves garlic, thinly sliced

1 small red bell pepper, cored, seeded, and thinly sliced

1 tablespoon grated lemon zest

2 tablespoons honey

2 tablespoons fresh rosemary, crumbled

Pinch of saffron

1/4 cup dry white wine, plus more as needed

16 asparagus spears

Preheat the oven to 350° F.

Rinse the chicken pieces under cold water. Pat dry. Season with salt and pepper.

In a large skillet, heat the olive oil over medium heat. Sauté the chicken until seared and golden on all sides, about ten minutes. Remove the chicken from the skillet and place in a nine-by-twelve-inch baking pan. Set aside.

In the same skillet, coated with flavorful cooking oil, sauté the onion, garlic, and red pepper. Cook over medium heat until the vegetables are softened, about three minutes. Scatter the sizzling sauté over the browned chicken.

In a small saucepan, combine the lemon zest, honey, rosemary, saffron, and white wine. Stir to mix well and warm over low heat until all the herbs are evenly incorporated with the honey, about two minutes. Keep the temperature as low as possible to avoid bruising the delicate flavor of the honey.

Pour the glaze evenly over the chicken and vegetables. Bake, uncovered, for forty minutes. Every fifteen minutes or so, baste with the juicy glaze. Feel free to add white wine as needed to keep the basting liquid plentiful.

Wash and trim the asparagus spears.

In the final fifteen minutes of baking, remove the pan from the oven to add the asparagus. Arrange the spears around the chicken to bake in the succulent juices.

Serve the chicken topped with honey-glazed vegetables and a fan of roasted asparagus.

Africa

MOROCCO

Lemon Chicken And Olives

~ classic complements ~

A LA CARTE

Roasted Eggplant Soup

Vegetable Couscous

Orange & Radish Salad

Thé de Menthe

Lemon Chicken And Olives

Zesty lemons and pungent olives make this chicken dish lusty and luscious. Slowly stewing the robust purple olives and the sunny lemon wedges releases their distinctive flavors to be beautifully absorbed by the chicken. The lemons become bittersweet and as soft as butter.

M A K E S   F O U R   S E R V I N G S

3 1/2-pound frying chicken, cut into eight pieces

3 tablespoons olive oil

1 large onion, thinly sliced

2 cloves garlic, minced

1/2-inch piece fresh ginger, peeled

1/4 cup chopped fresh parsley

2 tablespoons chopped cilantro

1 teaspoon salt

1/2 teaspoon freshly ground black pepper

Pinch of saffron

1 1/2 lemons, cut into 12 wedges

1/3 cup Kalamata olives, pitted

Rinse the chicken under cold water. Pat dry.

In a heavy-bottomed pot with a tightly fitting lid, heat the oil over medium heat. Sauté the chicken, turning frequently, until golden brown on all sides, about ten minutes.

Add the onion, garlic, ginger, half the parsley, the cilantro, salt, pepper, and saffron. Toss together to coat the chicken well. Cook for five minutes, or until the garlic is golden brown and the onion is soft.

Place the lemon wedges evenly over the chicken. Cover the pot, reduce the heat to low, and simmer for one and a half hours. Every fifteen minutes or so, as the chicken slowly simmers, baste and stir to evenly distribute the flavorful juices.

In the last fifteen minutes of cooking, add the olives. Cover and continue to cook until the chicken is very tender and the lemon wedges are stewed to buttery softness.

Carefully remove the chicken and lemon wedges from the pot. Place the chicken on a serving platter and surround with the wedges of lemon. Top with the olives and onions and cover to keep warm.

Raise the heat under the pot to medium and simmer the lemony juices until they thicken to a glaze, about five minutes. Pour the aromatic juices over the chicken and lemons, and garnish with the remaining parsley.

EGYPT

Phyllo Torte
~ classic complements ~
A LA CARTE

*Mezze Platter Of Stuffed Grape Leaves,
Hummus, Tabbouleh, And Baba Ghanoush*

Roasted Red Pepper & Pomegranate Salad

Fig Compote With Apricot Sorbet

Phyllo Torte

Savory custard, toasted almonds, and tender morsels of chicken spiced sweet and salty are sandwiched between layers of flaky phyllo dough. The centerpiece of a lavish Egyptian banquet, this wonderful pie is an exotic eating adventure.

M A K E S   S I X   S E R V I N G S

3 1/2-pound frying chicken, quartered

2 cups water

Medium onion, finely chopped

1/2 teaspoon ground ginger

1/2 teaspoon ground allspice

1/4 teaspoon powdered saffron

Salt and freshly ground black pepper to taste

1/4 cup fresh parsley sprigs, finely chopped

1 teaspoon ground cinnamon

6 large eggs

1 cup blanched almonds, finely chopped

12 tablespoons butter, melted

16 sheets phyllo dough

1 tablespoon sugar

1 egg yolk, beaten

Powdered sugar and ground cinnamon, for garnish

Rinse the chicken pieces under cold water.

In a large heavy-bottomed pot, simmer the water. Add the chicken and cook for about three minutes. Add the onion, ginger, allspice, saffron, salt, pepper, parsley, and one-half teaspoon cinnamon. Simmer, covered, for an hour and a half. Add water if necessary. Carefully remove the tender chicken and set aside to cool.

Pour the stock into a heatproof glass measuring cup. Strain a half cup into a small saucepan. Beat in the eggs, one at a time, until thoroughly blended. Add salt and pepper to taste. Cook, stirring, over low heat until the mixture is the consistency of creamy custard, about three minutes. Set aside.

Skin, bone, and slice the chicken into one-inch pieces. Set aside.

In a small saucepan, lightly toast the chopped almonds in two tablespoons of melted butter. Let cool.

Preheat the oven to 350° F.

Butter a thirteen-inch pie pan. Place a sheet of phyllo in the bottom with its edges hanging over the rim on all sides. Brush with melted butter. Cover with a second sheet. Brush with melted butter. Repeat this process four more times.

Sprinkle the sugar, the half-teaspoon cinnamon, and the toasted almonds on top. Evenly spread on two thirds of the custard. Drizzle with chicken stock. Cover with four buttered sheets of phyllo. Top with a neat layer of chicken. Evenly spread on the remaining custard. Drizzle with chicken stock. Cover with six more layers of buttered phyllo.

Pinch the overhanging edges of dough to seal securely around the rim. Brush the top with beaten egg yolk to glaze.

Bake for forty-five minutes. Then raise the temperature to 425° F. Bake for fifteen minutes, or until the pastry turns golden brown. Dust with powdered sugar and cinnamon. Cool for ten minutes before slicing and serving.

Asia

INDIA

Chicken Curry
~classic complements~

A LA CARTE

Vegetable Pakoras

Cucumber Raita & Tamarind Chutney

Carrot Halvah

Cardamom Lemon Fizz

Chicken Curry

Curry comes from a family reunion of fragrant spices that are the hallmark flavors of Indian cuisine. Cumin, coriander, and turmeric by themselves are bold and distinctive, but combined in a wonderful curry blend, they become miraculously subtle and balanced. That's the mystery and the magic of curry.

M A K E S   F O U R   S E R V I N G S

2 chicken breasts	1/2 teaspoon salt
3 cloves garlic	1 teaspoon ground cumin
1 large onion	1 teaspoon ground coriander
1 medium tomato	1 teaspoon ground turmeric
1-inch piece fresh ginger	1/2 cup plain yogurt
1 small serrano chili	2 tablespoons chopped
2 tablespoons peanut oil	cilantro, for garnish

Rinse the chicken under cold water. Pat dry.

Skin and bone the breasts. Slice the meat into two-inch cubes.

The best way to stir-fry efficiently is to prepare all the ingredients beforehand and arrange them within easy reach of the wok or skillet.

Peel and mince the cloves of garlic.

Thinly slice the onion.

Coarsely dice the tomatoes.

Peel and finely mince the ginger.

Remove the seeds from the chilies and mince. Or, include some of the seeds to give the curry extra zing. Be careful. The seeds pack a punch.

In a wok or large skillet, heat the oil over high heat until the oil is smoking hot. Add the garlic. Sauté until golden, about one minute. Add the onions and stir-fry until softened, about two minutes.

Turn up the heat slightly. Add the chicken cubes and cook, stirring rapidly, until they lose their pink color and begin to sear, about two minutes.

Add the tomato, salt, ginger, cumin, coriander, turmeric, and minced serrano chili. Stir-fry to mix well and to coat the chicken evenly. Lower the heat and simmer for five minutes.

Slowly add the yogurt to the skillet or wok. Tossing and stirring until well combined and all the ingredients are evenly coated. As you stir, the curry sauce emits a heavenly aroma and turns velvety smooth. Cover the skillet and simmer over very low heat for twenty minutes.

Mound the melt-in-your-mouth chicken curry in a large serving bowl. Decorate with a shower of cilantro.

THAILAND

Lemongrass Chicken

~ classic complements ~

A LA CARTE

Chilled Cilantro Soup

Green Mango Salad

Pad Thai

White Iced Coffee

Lemongrass Chicken

Chili lovers adore Thai-style Lemongrass Chicken, and with good reason! The chilies — con semias — give this colorful stir-fry its tastebud-tingling edge. Balance the heat with sweet coconut milk, sour spikes of lemongrass, and tart lime zest.

M A K E S   S I X   S E R V I N G S

3 1/2-pound frying chicken, cut into 8 pieces

1-inch piece fresh ginger

2 serrano chilies

3 lemongrass stalks

3 cups canned coconut milk

1 cup water

2 tablespoons peanut oil

1/2 teaspoon freshly ground black pepper

1 teaspoon salt

1 tablespoon grated lime zest

1/4 teaspoon kaffir lime powder

1 tablespoon *nam pla* (Asian fish sauce)

Juice of 1 lime

1/4 cup cilantro leaves, for garnish

Rinse the chicken pieces under cold water. Pat dry. Cut the chicken breasts in half. Set aside.

Lemongrass Chicken, like its sister recipe Chicken Curry, is a stir-fry. Take the time to manicure the vegetables and herbs in advance for best results.

Peel and thinly slice the ginger.

Mince the chilies, including the seeds.

Cut away the grassy tops of the lemongrass to leave stalks about six inches long. Peel away the tough outer leaves. Bruise the stalks with the blunt side of a heavy knife. Slice each stalk into four pieces. Set aside.

In a small glass bowl, combine one and a half cups of the coconut milk and the water. Stir to blend completely. Set aside.

Place a wok or large skillet over high heat. Add the oil. When the oil is hot, stir-fry the chicken pieces until seared on all sides, about five minutes.

Add the lemongrass, ginger, coconut milk mixture, pepper and salt , lime zest, lime powder, and chilies. Bring the liquid to a boil.

Reduce the heat to low and simmer, stirring occasionally, until the chicken is tender and the liquid is reduced by half, about thirty minutes.

Add the remaining one and a half cups coconut milk. Raise the heat to high and bring to a boil, stirring constantly. As soon as the liquid starts to bubble, remove from the heat and stir in the *nam pla* and the lime juice.

Arrange the chicken on a serving platter. Garnish with fragrant cilantro leaves.

CHINA

Bon Bon Chicken Salad

~ classic complements ~

A LA CARTE

Green Onion Pancakes

Fuzzy Melon Soup

Dwarf Vegetables With Five-Spice Sauce

Chrysanthemum Tea

Bon Bon Chicken Salad

The Chinese believe that long noodles ensure a long life and chicken guarantees renewed prosperity. We are more likely to combine foods simply for the pleasure good flavor gives us. Bon Bon Chicken Salad is so deliciously creamy, it's practically dessert. The scrumptious sesame sauce, the snap of the fresh green beans, and the mellow moistness of cold chicken are all the reasons you need to enjoy it heartily.

M A K E S   F O U R   S E R V I N G S

2 chicken breasts

2 cups water

6 scallions, white parts only

1-inch piece fresh ginger

1 1/2 cups green beans, trimmed

1 tablespoon Asian sesame oil

2 ounces mung bean cellophane noodles

1 tablespoon peanut oil

1 teaspoon grated fresh ginger

2 cloves garlic, minced

3 tablespoons Asian sesame paste

3 tablespoons soy sauce

2 tablespoons white wine vinegar

1 tablespoon sugar

1 tablespoon Asian hot chili pepper oil

1 tablespoon sesame seeds, toasted

Rinse the chicken breasts under cold water.

In a heavy-bottomed pot, simmer the water. Add the chicken breasts, three scallions, and the piece of ginger. Cook, partially covered, for fifteen minutes. Remove from the heat, cover the pot, and steep the chicken for thirty minutes.

Blanch the green beans in boiling water for thirty seconds. Rinse under cold water and drain. Slice on the diagonal into two-and-a-half-inch lengths.

Remove the poached breasts from the pot. Set aside to cool. Reserve three tablespoons of poaching liquid. Skin the breasts and rub with the sesame oil. Refrigerate, uncovered, until chilled. In a glass bowl, cover the noodles with very hot water to rehydrate until soft, about five minutes. Drain.

Bring a large pot of water to a boil. Add the noodles, reduce the heat to medium, and cook for five minutes. Drain and rinse under cold water. Place in a glass bowl and refrigerate, uncovered, until chilled.

In a small saucepan, combine the peanut oil, grated ginger, and garlic. Sauté over low heat until fragrant. Remove from the heat. Stir in the sesame paste, soy sauce, vinegar, sugar, chili pepper oil, and reserved poaching liquid. Stir well to dissolve the sugar and blend the sesame paste and spices. Set aside to cool to room temperature.

Bone the cold chicken breasts. Shred the meat into quarter-inch-wide slivers.

Slice the remaining three scallions lengthwise in half. They will fall apart into slivers.

Mound the chilled noodles on a serving platter. Arrange the green beans on top. Scatter the shredded chicken over all and dress generously with the sauce. Garnish with the scallion slivers and sesame seeds.

JAPAN

Yakitori Chicken

~ classic complements ~

A LA CARTE

Shrimp Gyoza With Vinegar Dipping Sauce

Sesame Spinach & Ginger Salad

Green Tea Ice Cream

Hot Sake

Yakitori Chicken

Yakitori-style grill cuisine is the best loved of its kind in Japan and here, too. Yakitori is the basting and dipping sauce that goes with delightful broiled or barbecued kebabs. As a basting liquid, the yakitori concentrates the natural goodness of the chicken and vegetables. As a traditional dipping sauce, it spikes every mouthful with extra flavor.

M A K E S   F O U R   S E R V I N G S

4 chicken legs with thighs	12 small mushrooms
Sixteen 12-inch-long bamboo skewers	2/3 cup sake
	1/4 cup mirin (sweet sake)
8 chicken livers	1/3 cup dark brown sugar
1 green bell pepper	1 cup soy sauce
8 scallions, white part only	2 tablespoons tamari

Preheat the oven to 350° F.

Rinse the chicken under cold water.

Skin and bone the chicken. Reserve one leg bone for flavoring the sauce.

Roast the leg bone until browned and crisp, about thirty minutes. Set aside.

Soak the bamboo skewers in water for fifteen minutes to prevent the ends from catching on fire during broiling.

Rinse the chicken livers under cold water. Pat dry. Slice in half.

Seed the bell pepper and slice into one-inch pieces.

Slice the scallions into one-inch lengths.

Cut the chicken meat into one-and-a-half-inch cubes.

Remove the stems from the mushroom caps and discard them.

Thread the chicken cubes, chicken livers, and vegetables onto the skewers, alternating the ingredients. Place the skewers in a large broiling pan. Set aside.

In a medium saucepan, combine the sake, mirin, brown sugar, soy sauce, and tamari. Stir briskly to mix well. Add the roasted leg bone. Simmer over medium heat until the sugar has dissolved and the sauce has reduced by half.

Remove the saucepan from the heat and let cool to room temperature.

Discard the leg bone and strain the yakitori sauce into a glass bowl.

Preheat the broiler.

Brush each skewer with the sauce. Place the broiling pan three inches from the heat, and broil for four minutes. Turn the skewers over. Baste with the sauce and broil until the chicken and vegetables are tender, about four minutes. Baste once more.

Transfer the remaining yakitori sauce to a small saucepan and bring just to a boil. Remove from the heat.

Arrange the skewers on a serving platter and brush again with the sauce.

Pour the yakitori sauce into small bowls, placed strategically for on-site dipping.

The Americas

BRAZIL

Chicken Beer Bake

~ classic complements ~

A LA CARTE

Grilled Sausages & Black Olives

Couve Collard Greens

Black Beans & Saffron Rice

Sweet Corn Flan

Chicken Beer Bake

Delicate young broilers soak up the dramatic flavors from a Brazilian beer bath of syrupy dark ale, a trio of pungent herbs, and hot pepper flakes. Though marinating requires preplanning, it does not require vigilance to make the dish taste as though it's been cooking for hours. This savory chicken comes together with ease.

M A K E S   F O U R   S E R V I N G S

Two 2-pound broiling chickens, cut in half

1 medium onion, thinly sliced

Two 12-ounce bottles dark ale

1 tablespoon chopped garlic

1 tablespoon dried oregano

1 tablespoon dried tarragon

2 teaspoons dried basil

1 tablespoon paprika

1/2 teaspoon freshly ground black pepper

1/2 teaspoon red pepper flakes

1 teaspoon kosher salt

Rinse the chickens under cold water. Pat dry.

Arrange the chicken skin side down in a roasting pan. Spread the onion rings over the chicken. Add the beer, and evenly distribute the garlic, oregano, tarragon, basil, paprika, black pepper, red pepper flakes, and salt over the chicken. Cover the pan with foil. Marinate in the refrigerator for at least two hours, or preferably overnight. The longer the poultry and onion rings marinate, the more flavorful the results.

Bring the chicken to room temperature before baking. Preheat the oven to 400° F.

Cover the roasting pan with fresh foil. Bake for one and a half hours. Remove the foil and turn the chicken over to brown the skin. Stir the cooking liquid and turn the onion rings. Continue to bake for fifteen minutes.

Remove the chicken and onion rings from the pan and arrange them on an ovenproof serving platter. Keep warm in a 100° F. oven, or the lowest setting, while you transform the cooking juices into a glaze.

Place the roasting pan on top of the stove. Bring the liquid to a boil over high heat and cook until the juices are reduced by half, about eight minutes. Stir vigorously several times to scrape up the delicious bits of chicken clinging to the bottom of the pan.

Remove the chicken and onion rings from the oven and spoon a generous amount of beer sauce over all.

MEXICO

Chicken Mole

~classic complements~

A LA CARTE

Pozole

Jicama & Spicy Watermelon Salad

Chocolate Bread Pudding

Cold Mexican Beer

Chicken Mole

Pour on a generous amount of rich-as-velvet mole to dress up simply prepared chicken breasts. The complex taste of chocolate, chilies, and aromatic spices gives Mexico's premier celebration sauce a pungent, full flavor for a festive menu any time of year.

M A K E S   S I X   S E R V I N G S

2 dried pasilla chilies, seeded

3 dried ancho chilies, seeded

3 dried mulato chilies, seeded

3 chicken breasts, skinned, and cut in half

2 cups water

1 1/2 onions, coarsely chopped

7 cloves garlic, peeled

1/2 teaspoon salt

2 tablespoons vegetable oil

2 medium tomatoes, chopped

6 canned tomatillos, drained, chopped

1/3 cup unsalted roasted peanuts

1/3 cup blanched almonds

1 teaspoon whole cloves

1 teaspoon ground cinnamon

1/2 teaspoon anise seeds

4 black peppercorns

1/3 cup raisins

3 ounces unsweetened chocolate

1 tablespoon sugar

1/2 cup toasted sesame seeds

Cilantro sprigs for garnish

Place the dried chilies in a glass bowl. Cover with very hot water. Rehydrate until soft, about thirty minutes.

Rinse the chicken breasts under cold water.

Place the breasts in a large pot. Add the water, one-half

cup of the chopped onions, two cloves garlic, and the salt. Simmer, covered, until the chicken is tender, about twenty minutes. Remove the chicken from the broth and set aside.

Pour the broth through a strainer into a glass bowl and set aside. Discard the onions and garlic.

Heat the oil in a skillet over medium heat. Add the tomatoes, tomatillos, and the remaining onions and garlic. Sauté for three minutes, stirring well. Transfer to a blender or food processor. Add the peanuts, almonds, cloves, cinnamon, anise seeds, peppercorns, raisins, and softened chilies, along with their liquid. Blend to a fine puree.

In a large skillet, combine the spicy puree, reserved chicken broth, the chocolate, and the sugar. Cook, stirring, until the chocolate has melted and the sauce is velvety smooth. Cover, lower the heat, and simmer the melt-in-your-mouth mole sauce for twenty minutes. Add the chicken breasts and simmer to reheat them, about ten minutes.

Transfer the chicken mole to a large serving platter, sprinkle with the sesame seeds, and garnish with lots of fresh cilantro sprigs.

JAMAICA

Burning Spear Chicken

~ classic complements ~

A LA CARTE

Panfried Sweet Plantains

Tamarind Banana Chutney

Rice & Peas

Limed Papaya & Mango Fresca

Burning Spear Chicken

The super-spiced "burning spear" flavor can travel. As an alfresco alternative to using a vertical roaster or rotisserie at home, bring the bird to the beach! The thick marinade paste really stands up to grilling over a bed of glowing coals.

MAKES FOUR SERVINGS

3 1/2-pound roasting chicken

1 tablespoon dried minced onion

1 tablespoon onion powder

2 teaspoons dried thyme

1 teaspoon salt

1 teaspoon ground allspice

1/4 teaspoon ground nutmeg

1/4 teaspoon ground cinnamon

2 teaspoons sugar

1 teaspoon coarsely ground black pepper

1 teaspoon cayenne pepper

2 teaspoons dried minced chives

2 whole scallions, finely chopped

1 small onion, finely chopped

2 tablespoons freshly squeezed lime juice

1 tablespoon hot pepper sauce

Rinse the chicken under cold water. Pat dry. Set aside.

In a blender or food processor, combine the dried onion, onion powder, thyme, salt, allspice, nutmeg, cinnamon, sugar, black pepper, cayenne pepper, chives, scallions, onion, lime juice, and hot pepper sauce. Blend to a thick paste to yield about a half cup.

Place the chicken, breast side up, on a work surface.

Gently pull the skin away from the breast meat. Slide two tablespoons of the marinade paste under the skin with your fingers. Turn the bird over to rest, breast side down, and gently pull the skin away from the back. Slide two more tablespoons of paste underneath. Smear the remaining paste inside the cavity and over the outside of the chicken to coat completely. Set aside at room temperature for an hour or so to allow the spices to permeate the meat.

Preheat the oven to 350° F.

Place the chicken on a vertical roaster, then set the roaster in a pan to catch the precious drippings as the bird cooks. (If you don't own a vertical roaster, roast the bird in the traditional way — in a medium roasting pan.) Roast in the oven for one hour and fifteen minutes (about twenty minutes per pound). When done to a turn, the internal temperature at the thickest part of the thigh should be 165° F. and the skin crackling crisp with a rich mahogany crust.

Remove the chicken from the oven and let it cool for about ten minutes before removing it from the roaster.

Carve the bird into eight serving pieces — drumsticks, thighs, breasts, and wings. Arrange the chicken on a large serving platter and be prepared for a heat wave!

LOUISIANA

Chicken Gumbo

~ classic complements ~

A LA CARTE

Pineapple Sorbet

Okra Sticks

Dirty Rice

Praline Pie

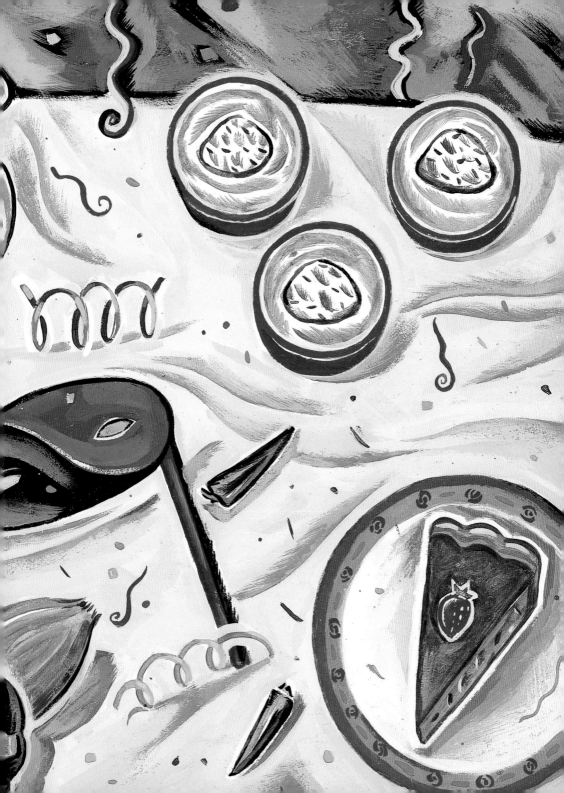

Chicken Gumbo

Everything that's special about Cajun cooking is in the back-country soup called gumbo. At the heart of this recipe is the classic preparation of the roux, a technique probably brought over from France hundreds of years ago. The sautéed seasoned flour with its rousing robust tang hasn't lost its flavorful authority or changed much since the days of the first Louisianians.

M A K E S   S I X   S E R V I N G S

3 1/2-pound frying chicken, cut into 8 pieces

1 1/4 cups all-purpose flour

Salt and freshly ground black pepper to taste

1 teaspoon garlic powder

1 teaspoon cayenne pepper

Vegetable oil for frying

1 medium onion, finely chopped

1 green bell pepper, cored, seeded, and finely chopped

2 celery stalks, finely chopped

6 cups chicken stock

1/2 pound andouille sausage, cut into 1/4-inch rounds

2 cloves garlic, minced

Rinse the chicken pieces under cold water. Pat dry.

In a glass bowl, combine the flour, salt and pepper, garlic powder, and cayenne pepper. Set aside one-half cup of the seasoned flour.

Place the remaining flour mixture and the chicken in a paper bag. Shake vigorously to coat the chicken.

In a large heavy-bottomed skillet, heat a half inch of oil to almost smoking. Fry the chicken for about twenty-five minutes, turning frequently to brown nicely on all sides. Drain on paper towels.

Carefully pour the hot cooking fat into a glass measuring cup, leaving the flavorful bits of browned chicken in the skillet.

Return one-half cup of the oil to the skillet. Raise the heat to high. Whisk in the reserved seasoned flour and cook, whisking constantly, until the roux turns a dark red-brown, about four minutes. (For ease and safety, use a long-handled whisk.) Be careful not to let the super-hot oil splash on your skin.

Turn off the heat. Quickly stir in the onion, bell pepper, and celery, and continue to stir, until the roux is almost black, about two minutes. Turn the heat back on to low and sauté the roux-blackened vegetables until soft. As you sauté, stir constantly to scrape up the tasty tidbits stuck to the bottom of the pan. Remove from the heat.

In a large saucepan, bring the chicken stock to a boil. Add the roux-coated vegetables, a spoonful at a time. Turn down the heat to low. Add the sausage and garlic. Simmer, uncovered, for forty minutes.

Skin and debone the chicken. Cut the meat into one-inch pieces. Stir the chicken chunks into the gumbo. Taste for salt and pepper and adjust the seasoning, if necessary. Ladle the spicy gumbo into six wide shallow bowls.

KENTUCKY

Fried Chicken With Gravy

~ classic complements ~

A LA CARTE

Mostly Corn Succotash

Apple & Chicory Slaw

Peach Shortcake

Spearmint Lemonade

Fried Chicken With Gravy

No dish exemplifies American home cooking more perfectly than Southern-fried chicken with gravy. My husband's family hails from the South, and this tried-and-true recipe has been handed down from generation to generation, picking up culinary idiosyncrasies along the way. My contribution is a buttermilk marinade to ensure succulence in every crunchy bite.

MAKES FOUR SERVINGS

3 1/2 pound frying chicken, cut into eight pieces	2 teaspoons freshly ground black pepper
2 cups buttermilk	3 cups vegetable oil
1 cup plus 2 tablespoons self-rising flour	3/4 cup chicken stock
2 teaspoons salt	1/4 cup heavy cream

Rinse the chicken pieces under cold water. Pat dry.

Arrange the chicken in a single layer in a baking dish. Pour the buttermilk over the chicken. Place in the refrigerator to marinate for thirty minutes.

Season one cup of the flour with the salt and pepper. Put the seasoned flour in a paper bag. Add the buttermilk-coated chicken and shake vigorously to coat each piece with flour.

Heat a cast-iron skillet over medium-high heat. Choose a skillet that's roomy enough to fit the chicken close together, but not touching. Add the vegetable oil and heat to 340° F. Three cups of vegetable oil in a twelve-inch skillet reaches a perfect frying depth of a half inch.

Remove the chicken from the bag, shake each piece gently to dislodge any excess flour, and arrange in the skillet. To guarantee golden-brown crispness on all sides, turn the chicken frequently with tongs to protect the skin from punctures. Fry, uncovered, for ten to fifteen minutes.

Lower the heat and continue to cook, partially covered, until the chicken is tender, about ten minutes more. The total cooking time for deliciously tender fried chicken is twenty-five minutes.

Remove the chicken from the skillet. Place the chicken on paper towels to absorb any excess cooking oil before transferring to a large serving platter.

To make the gravy, pour off all but three tablespoons of the pan drippings. Set the pan over low heat, sprinkle in the remaining two tablespoons of flour and cook, stirring constantly, for two minutes. Add the chicken stock and cream. Cook until the gravy thickens, about three minutes. Pour it piping hot into a gravy boat, ready to dress the platter of crispy fried chicken waiting at the table.

CALIFORNIA

Free-Range Chicken In Paper

~ classic complements ~

A LA CARTE

Cold Sun-Dried Tomato Soup

Longevity Salad Of Baby Lettuces & Sprouts

Grilled Fruit Kebabs With Kiwi Puree

Napa Wine Spritzer

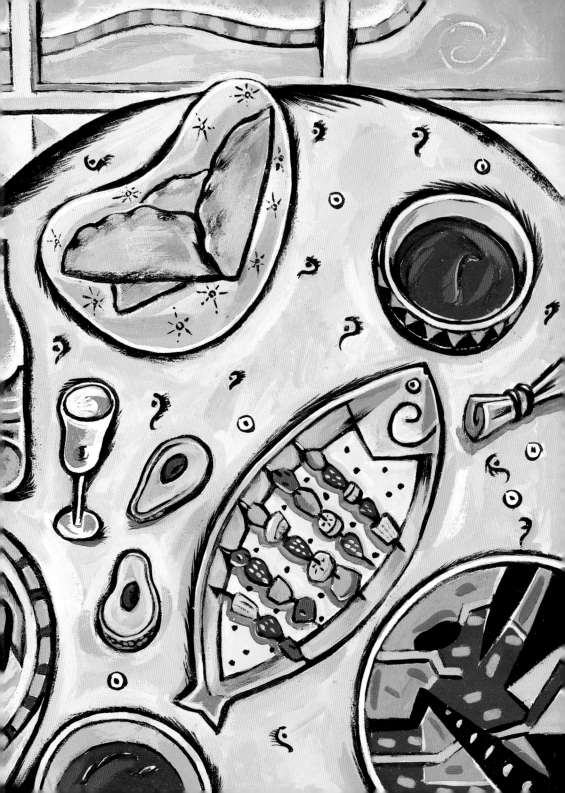

Free-Range Chicken In Paper

Get down to basics and "good" food — skinless white-meat chicken, the freshest garden-grown ingredients, a drizzle of olive oil — to begin eating right, eating less, and feeling better. This dish is a great example of New World Order Cuisine. The flavorful chicken, ripe tomatoes, and tart olives, seasoned with thyme, orange zest, and shallots, are steamed in paper packets for a bright, clear taste.

MAKES FOUR SERVINGS

2 skinless, boneless, free-range chicken breasts

Salt and freshly ground black pepper to taste

2 teaspoons olive oil

4 large cloves garlic, peeled

Four 11- by 18-inch sheets parchment paper

2 tablespoons unsalted butter, melted

2 shallots, peeled and thinly sliced

2 plum tomatoes, sliced

1 tablespoon grated orange zest

4 sprigs fresh thyme

8 oil-cured olives, pitted

2 tablespoons freshly squeezed orange juice

Rinse the chicken under cold water. Pat dry. Cut each in half to make four half breasts. Season with salt and pepper and set aside.

Preheat the oven to 375° F.

In a small frying pan, heat one teaspoon of the oil. Sauté

the garlic until dark gold on all sides, about two minutes. Set aside.

To prepare the parchment pouches, fold each piece of paper crosswise, in half, to make a crease. Open them up to lay flat. Brush the inside with the melted butter.

Position a seasoned chicken breast on each sheet about two inches below the centerfold. Divide the garlic, shallots, tomatoes, orange zest, thyme, and olives evenly among the chicken breasts, arranging them around the chicken. Sprinkle with the orange juice and drizzle the remaining one teaspoon olive oil over all.

Fold the top of each sheet over the ingredients. Fold over about a quarter inch of the edges along the three open sides. Then fold the edges over a second time to seal the pouch securely.

Arrange the pouches on a baking sheet. Bake until the pouches puff up and the paper is slightly brown, about fifteen to twenty minutes.

With a sharp knife, cut a slit in the center of each pouch to allow the steam to escape. Place a hot pouch on each dinner plate.

Eat the tender chicken and tart vegetables right out of the browned paper packets.